OF THINGS UNSEEN
...AND OTHER POEMS

OF THINGS UNSEEN
...AND OTHER POEMS

LEE BAIN CHIARO

Writers Club Press
New York Lincoln Shanghai

Of Things Unseen…and Other Poems

Writers Club Press
an imprint of iUniverse, Inc.

For information address:
iUniverse
2021 Pine Lake Road, Suite 100
Lincoln, NE 68512
www.iuniverse.com

ISBN: 0-595-25611-2 (Pbk)
ISBN: 0-595-65211-5 (Cloth)

Printed in the United States of America

Lord, help me to honor Christ this day
in all I do, in all I say;
O make me become a fisher of men *
'though all I have in my hand is a pen.
Amen, Amen!

Matthew 4:19

CONTENTS

PREFACE

I cannot recall the year, but it was while I was still young…probably in my late twenties, that the Voice of the Lord spoke to my heart. I was lying across my bed one evening, contemplating my troubled life, when I distinctly heard these words: **"I Am the God of Abraham, the God of Isaac, the God of Jacob. I have given you a gift. You must never use this gift for your own profit, but you must share it with others."** As gentle tears began to course down my cheeks, I vowed to obey His words.

I did not dare to tell anyone that God had spoken to me, because everyone would have thought that I had taken leave of my senses. In fact, prior to this experience, I, too, did not know that God still speaks to people today.

As the busy years went by, the memory of this incident faded. I kept sending my poetry, which was mainly romantic and secular at that time, to various publications at the urging of my friends. However, as the rejection slips became more numerous, I began to ponder the reason.

Many years later, after I had accepted Messiah Jesus as my Savior, The Holy Spirit of the Living God brought to my remembrance the covenant I had made with Him years earlier.

I told the Lord how greatly I regretted having forgotten my promise, and thereafter kept my poetry, which was now spiritual in nature and dedicated to Him, in a notebook. If He wanted to keep my light under a bushel, so be it.

More years elapsed before my dear daughter, Jodi, decided to give me a unique Mother's Day gift. She proposed putting my poetry into book form. I was delighted beyond words! I called the little book, *Beauty for Ashes*, after *Isaiah 61:3*. Another book went into print a few years later, called *The Still, Small Voice*.

Through these books, and my Testimony, *Forbidden Quest*, I began to share the gift the Lord had given me, just as He had said. The poems seemed to bless everyone who read or heard them. Proceeds from their sale go to the Benevolence Fund of our Church.

Of Things Unseen...and Other Poems

In 1996 I began presenting Scriptural teachings to the congregation at Family Worship Center, and accompanied the readings with the poems they had inspired. I am still sharing this gift with others. Once again my daughter, bless her, has encouraged me to put the teachings, along with the poems, into book form.

That is how the book you are holding came into being. May it bless you and encourage you. This is my prayer. Amen.

Lee Bain Chiaro
July 6, 2002

ACKNOWLEDGMENT

I would like to thank my dear friend, Blanche M. Novak,
who introduced me to my Messiah…The One Who is ever my Inspiration.

LEGACY

To my children, grandchildren, and great-grandchildren:

O let me leave a legacy of Love
when from this woeful world I shall depart;
possessing neither gold nor priceless art,
I must bequeath to you my treasure trove
of simpler gifts: thoughts from the heart.

Take, then this volume of my verse
and trace therein the Truths I've learned
through all my sufferings and pain…
and may you glean still greater gain
therefrom than I myself have earned.

October 4, 1968

Hymn to The Infinite

Since first I glimpsed
Invisible Things…

fell at the feet
of the King of Kings…

sated my thirst
at His Sacred Springs …

and thrilled to the strains
of Celestial Strings;

I yearn to shed dread earthly things,
and cling to those Eternal Things
to which my singing spirit wings!

May 12, 1978

SURRENDER

He asked me only to believe
the unbelievable:
He asked that I perceive
the inconceivable:
that Christ Is, Was, and Ever Will Be.

He knocked, then bade me let Him enter;
He sought a seat at my life's center…
to make my lonely heart His dwelling;
to fill it full to swelling
with His Love compelling.

Throughout Life's course
I fought the force
of His entreating…
'though oft He spoke
in moments fleeting…
the same, soft plea
came He repeating.

Vainly I had sought some measure
of the world's elusive pleasure…
but the joys of life were fading;
laughter played strange games
evading me.

He asked me to believe that He
would meet my needs, whate'er they be.
Wearily I leaned, then acquiesced,
and finally, His Name be Blessed,
I yielded all my life, my soul,
and, in so doing, was made whole!

December 31, 1968

· 3 ·

Come Unto Me!

Whenever we ask people where they live, they might name a street, a part of town, or even a different city. But everyone can also have another address, a spiritual one, right here on earth!

Psalm 91:1 declares that "He who dwells in the secret place of the Most High, shall abide under the shadow of the Almighty."

Where is this secret place where we can live in confidence, security, and peace? And how can we find the way?

I'm glad you asked! Here's the good news: it is very near…as near as the sacred sanctuary of the seeking, praying, listening heart, hearing a quiet Voice saying, **"Be still and know that I Am God."** (*Psalm 46:10*)

Then, out of that stillness comes the Voice of the One who proclaimed, **"I Am the way, the Truth, and the Life; no one comes to the Father except through Me."**

And Christ's majestic message, found in *John's Gospel 14:6*, echoes ever afresh the *good news* that Almighty God will welcome us into the secret place of His Gracious Presence when, by Faith, we express our need for the cleansing power of the Holy Blood-Sacrifice of his Dear Son for our despicable sins.

For, without Faith it is impossible to please Him, because he who comes to God must believe that **He Is,** and that He is a rewarder of those who diligently seek Him (*Hebrews 11:6*).

And *Hebrews 9:22* explains that without the shedding of Sinless Blood there is no forgiveness for our rebellious sins.

So, in *Matthew 11:28*, Jesus calls each of us to come to Him and find rest for our troubled souls.

James 4:8 urges us to draw near to God, because when we do, He will draw near to us.

Christ assures us, in *John 6:37*, that if we come to Him, He will by no means cast us out and that no one will be able to snatch us out of His Hand.

Psalm 16:11 promises us that in His Presence is fullness of Joy: at His right hand there are pleasures forevermore.

And we find, when we approach Him, that He is always there, waiting for us with open arms, eager to draw us into the shelter of his tender, everlasting love, as in *Jeremiah 31:3*.

And this is how He drew me:

"Come Unto Me!" *

"Come unto me," Jesus beckoned;
"come unto me, I will give
comfort for all of your sorrows…
Joy, that you truly may live."

Hesitantly I approached Him,
shackled by fetters of fear;
but He continued his pleading…
and His wondrous words drew me near:

"Bring me your loss and your heartaches…
bring me your grief and your tears…
bring me the deep disappointments
that have wearied and withered your years."

Suddenly, no longer fearing,
I rushed to his spear-piercéd side,
and He, in sweetest compassion,
smiled and opened arms wide.

Entering His Presence I marveled
at the Love on His Glorious Face,
as He anointed with Joy my sorrow
in that Holy-of-Holiest Place.

March 17, 1977

*Matthew 11:28

INCARNATION

In the days when God's people
felt Rome's iron fist,
when none could deliver,
for none dared resist…
God's heart of Love
with compassion was moved…
setting in motion
The Plan He'd approved.

Then the Lord left the Heavens…
relinquished His Throne…
visited Earth
clothed in sinew and bone.

Came as a babe, helpless and sweet…
played, as a child, at His dear Mother's feet;
grew strong in stature, in Wisdom, and Grace,
and began to speak Peace
in that desolate place.

His miracle walk
among men had begun;
yet some refused to believe
He was truly God's Son.

In meekness He came,
seeking, by Grace,
to set all men free…
their sin to erase.

But man in his folly and unbelief
put Christ, The Messiah, to shame and to grief.

They despised the Redeemer…
rejected His Word;
turned a deaf ear
to the message they heard.
In exchange for His Love
returned scourge, nail, and thorn,
and laughed The Great King of Glory to scorn.

But His cruel Crucifixion
purchased our Peace,
with promise of Joys
that never shall cease.

Alive evermore,
Jesus beckons all men
to love and to serve Him
'til He comes once again.

Even so come, Lord Jesus! Amen and Amen.

December 25, 1982

John 1:1
John 1:14

My Answer

We rejoice today because it is written: "Unto us a child is born, unto us a Son is given. And the government, shall be upon his shoulder, and His Name shall be called Wonderful, Counselor, Mighty God, Everlasting Father, Prince of Peace!"

These familiar words from the Prophecy of *Isaiah 9:6* predict the coming of the Messiah of Israel...The Anointed One...who would save His people from sin and oppression.

When He finally arrived about 700 years later, the Apostle *John*, in the New Testament (*1:14*) proclaimed: "And the Word became flesh and dwelt among us, and we beheld His Glory...the Glory as of the only begotten of the Father, full of Grace and Truth."

Although Yeshuah (Jesus) came first to the House of Israel, most of His own people failed to recognize Him. But to those who did receive Him, both Jewish and Gentile, He gave the power to become the blood-bought children of Almighty God...of whom, by His Grace, I am one; Bless His Holy Name forever!

Why were my people unable to recognize their own Messiah? Here is my answer:

MY ANSWER

You asked me why my people rage
against The Christ of history's page…

They sought a king to conquer Rome…
a victor for the battle's fray…
a palace for his earthly home;
they found a babe on a bed of hay.

They sought a hero glorious, great
to end earth's reign of endless hate;
they only heard an infant's wail…
what could so frail a sound avail?

They sought a warrior girt with might
to put opposing force to flight;
they sought a leader valiant, strong,
but only heard a Mother's song.

Why did not God deign to present
His Son equipped with armament?
Instead that lonely, quiet morn
Messiah, unadorned, was born.

Why did God choose a tiny boy
to conquer sin, bring peace and joy?
I sought an answer to this plight
in deep despair, in darkest night.

My answer came one Christmas morn…
This is the reason Christ was born:

A conqueror could not quell my fears;
a monarch would not dry my tears;

a hero could not heal my heart;
a warrior could no peace impart.

Only a tender, gentle man,
sharing our humanity…
bearing His humility…
daring death to set us free…
was able to complete God's plan;
could comfort us and understand;
could wash us clean and make us strong,
and change our sighing into song;
could dry our tears and heal our heart,
and Joy and Peace and Love impart.

Thank you, Jesus. Amen.

December 14, 1979

THE ATONEMENT

I'd like to share with you some thoughts on the importance of the Atonement…Christ's Holy Sacrifice.

But first, we must revisit the Old Testament where we see Abraham, God's faithful servant, ready to sacrifice his beloved son, Isaac, in obedience to God's command.

This touching story is found in *Genesis 22:1-13*. There we find that at the last moment, God mercifully spared Isaac's life by providing a substitute to be slain…a ram caught by its horns in the thicket.

Then, in *Leviticus 17:11*, the Lord explains that "The Life of the flesh is in the blood…for it is the blood that makes atonement for the soul."

Although animal sacrifices were required of the people of Israel year after year, they could provide only a temporary covering for sin.

In *Hebrews 9:12-14*, the writer declares that animal blood could never purify our consciences. In *verse 22* of the same chapter, he adds: That without the shedding of blood, there is no forgiveness for sin, but it has to be Holy blood.

Then, in the prophetic book of *Isaiah 53:1-12*, we read the dreadful description of the crucifixion of the Messiah…Yeshuah…Jesus, the Lamb of God, who became our substitute by shedding his own Holy blood for our sins—once for all…giving eternal redemption…restoring us to God.

And now, in the Church, whenever we take communion, the bread and the cup are symbolic of the body and blood of our Savior, and with grateful hearts we remember again His sacred sacrifice…Bless His Holy Name!

According to *John 3:16*, God loved the world so much that He gave His only begotten Son, that whoever believes in Him should not perish, but have everlasting life!

2 Peter 3:9 tells us that "God is not willing that any should perish, but that all should come to repentance"…that is, to turn from our sins and to live for the risen Christ. Amen!

To help me to better understand the meaning of the Atonement, God's provision for the forgiveness of sin, the Lord graciously gave me these lines:

THE ATONEMENT

There was no ram in the thicket
when Christ, my Messiah, died
at the hands of the cruel and wicked,
by whose pride He was crucified.

No longer need rams' blood be proffered
to cover man's hideous sin,
since the Lamb of God Himself offered
to inflict our torment on Him.

For Abraham's son on the altar
God stayed the Death-Angel's hand;
yet the Son of God did not falter
in obeying Love's fatal demand.

Come, worship our Living Lord Jesus
for His merciful sacrifice!
By His Blood He purchased and freed us;
now we're destined for Paradise!

July 23, 1993

The Shadow   and   *The Substance*
Genesis 22:1-13   *John 3:16*
Leviticus 17:11   *Hebrews 9:12, 22*
Isaiah 53:1-12

Of Things Unseen

Let's take a little closer look at some invisible things:

In *Hebrews 11:1*, the writer declares: "Now Faith is the substance of things hoped for, the evidence of *things not seen*."

And in *1 Corinthians 2:9*, the Apostle *Paul* exclaims: "Eye has not seen...nor ear heard...neither have entered into the heart of man...the things God has prepared for those who love him."

Further, in *2 Corinthians 4:18*, *Paul* explains that, "We look not at the things which are seen, but at the things which are *not* seen...for the things which are seen are temporary, but the things which are not seen are eternal."

Then, in *1 Peter 1:8*, that Apostle writes of Jesus Christ: "Whom having not seen, you love...in whom, though now you see Him not...yet believing...you rejoice with joy unspeakable and full of Glory."

As I studied these scriptures, the Holy Spirit of God moved me to write these lines:

OF THINGS UNSEEN *

I love Him Whom I have not seen:
The Lord, Whom I adore!
On Arms Invisible I lean
that He may strength restore.

His soundless Voice speaks comfort sweet
to my world-weary heart;
I kneel before His nail-scarred feet
where daily cares depart.

'Though earthly eyes may see Him not,
I shall behold His Face;
mine is the soul His Blood has bought
by His Prevailing Grace.

The skeptic's mind requires a sign
before he will believe;
the heart of faith cries "He is mine!"
and Life Sublime receives.

With Joy unspeakable I'm stirred
to worship Christ my King;
while resting in His Precious Word,
to Unseen Hands I cling!

June 5, 1985

*Hebrews 11:1
2 Corinthians 4:18
1 Peter 1:8,9

BEAUTY FOR ASHES

We can truly rejoice today because it is written: "The Lord is Risen indeed!"

According to *Luke's Gospel 24:34*, and in *John's Gospel 11:25, 26*, the Lord Jesus declares: "**I am the Resurrection and the Life; he who believes in me, though he has died, yet shall he live and whoever lives and believes in me, shall never die!**" This is Christ's promise to us of eternal life and the source of our joy!

And He said: "**The words that I speak unto you, they are Spirit and they are life!**" *John 6:63.*

So that we may know that He alone can give and sustain life, Christ proclaimed: "**I am the Way, the Truth, and The Life. No one comes to the Father except through me.**" *John 14:6.*

Then in *John 14:19*, Jesus, the Lord of Life, reaffirms: "**Because I live, you shall live also.**"

And in *John 10:10*, speaking of believers, He said: "**I am come that they may have life, and that they may have it more abundantly.**"

Thanks be to God for His indescribable gift! (*2 Corinthians 9:15*)

And in the Old Testament, about 700 years before Messiah came to earth, the Prophet *Isaiah*, in *Chapter 61* told of an Anointed One who would…

> "Comfort all who mourn…
> Give beauty for ashes…
> The oil of Joy for mourning…
> And the garment of praise, for the spirit of heaviness."

Those wonderful words of hope prompted these words of mine:

BEAUTY FOR ASHES *

Beauty for ashes He brought me…
Sweet oil of Joy for my tears…
Anthems of Praise He has taught me,
to replace the pain of my years.

Comfort He brings to the broken,
this Healer of grief-stricken hearts;
by Blessed Words He has spoken,
Love, Joy, and Peace He imparts.

High Hope is He to the hopeless…
while souls bound by sin He sets free;
A Shelter of Rest for the homeless…
A Help to the helpless is He.

Healing He brings to the ailing,
yet even at death's final hour
He promises Life-Never-Failing,
for He is The Source of All Power.

Of Whom is my simple song singing…
this One Who gives Beauty for shame?
Messiah, to Whom I am clinging…
Christ Jesus, The Lord, is His Name!

September 14, 1984

*Isaiah 61:1-3

LOVE NOT THE WORLD

While searching the Scriptures, I discovered a lot of *let us* in my Bible. Not the salad kind, but the kind of *let us* that calls us to a deeper relationship with our Holy God and also with each other. So now, let us read some of these life-changing words.

Hebrews 10:22-24: "Let us draw near with a true heart, in full assurance of faith, having our hearts sprinkled from an evil conscience, and our bodies washed with pure water, let us hold fast the confession of our hope without wavering, for He who promised is faithful." (Amen!)

And "let us respect one another in order to stir up love and good works."

Hebrews 12:1b: "Let us lay aside every weight and the sin which so easily ensnares us and let us run with endurance the race that is set before us."

Hebrews 4:16: "Let us, therefore, come boldly to the Throne of Grace, that we may obtain mercy and find grace to help in time of need."

1 John 4:7, 8b: "Beloved, let us love one another, for love is of God, and everyone who loves, is born of God and knows God…for God is Love."

Galations 5:25, 26: "If we live in the Spirit, let us also walk in the Spirit, and let us not become conceited, provoking one another, envying one another."

Galations 6:9, 10: "And let us not grow weary while doing good, for in due season we shall reap if we do not lose heart. Therefore, as we have opportunity, let us do good to all, especially to those who are of the household of faith." (Amen!)

To help me in my own personal walk with the Lord, He led me to pen this prayer, many years before we ever heard of the World Wide Web. It is based on *1 John 2:15-17, Love Not the World*:

LOVE NOT THE WORLD *

Keep us, O Lord, from the web-of-the-world
that entices with sinuous thread;
'though this snare glistens silken, dew-pearled,
fill Christian hearts with its dread!

Help us, O Lord, to pursue wholly Thy Way…
righteous, victorious, and pure;
grant us the strength of Thy Spirit each day
to resist sin's fatal allure.

With heart's yielded to pleasing Thee,
we present this fervent request:
Help us to serve Thee obediently
and to triumph when put to the test.

Thus, when Life's race is finally run,
we'll receive our Blessed Reward:
hearing Jesus declare, "Servant, well done!"
as we enter The Joy of our Lord. Amen

January 23, 1984

*1 John 2:15-17

Arise, America!

Because God is Gracious, our nation will once again celebrate Independence Day. As you may know, I was not born in this country but came to America as a refugee from Nazi Germany.

As a naturalized citizen of the United States, I cherish the precious freedoms with which the Lord has blessed my beloved adopted country.

But how long will we remain *the Land of the Free and the Home of the Brave*?

Can a Holy God continue to bless a sinful nation?

The Lord gave me His answer by way of this poem, based on *Proverbs 14:34* and *Psalms 33:12*:

ARISE, AMERICA! *

The nation God chooses to honor
is the nation whose God is The Lord.
That nation is founded on Justice,
and exalts The Truth of His Word.

The crown of her glory is Freedom…
while beauty bespeaks her success…
her scepter extended in mercy…
this nation whom God seeks to bless.

With Virtue the source of her power,
the tempter's best test she withstands;
America, in this solemn hour,
our destiny rests in your hands!

For the nation God chooses to honor
is the nation whose God is the Lord;
that nation is founded on Justice,
and proclaims The Truth of His Word:

It is Written:

"Righteousness exalteth a nation; but sin is a
reproach to any people." (*Proverbs 14:34*)

"Blessed is the nation whose God is the Lord; and
the people whom He has chosen for His own
inheritance." (*Psalm 33:12*)

America, Arise!

April 12, 1982

* 1 Corinthians 15:34
Ephesians 5:14-17

ℱ౨

· 20 ·

Behold The Man!

How we enjoy hearing and singing our favorite melodies again and again! And, as believers, we also never tire of hearing the Good News: The Gospel of our Lord and Savior, Jesus Christ!

So, as we recall those earth-shaking events from Palm Sunday to the Crucifixion, Death, and Resurrection of our Gracious Lord, May God be Glorified, and may you be blessed! Amen.

BEHOLD THE MAN! *
A Passover Portrait **

The palms in the street
were fragrant and green;
His bearing was regal...
His manner serene.

His head seemed adorned
by invisible crown,
as the steps of the colt
led Jesus through town.

"Hosanna! Hosanna!"
Loud shouting and cheers
for the Son of David
rang in his ears.

How quickly was wrought
a change in this scene;
the crowd...now a mob;
the shouts...now a scream:

"Crucify! Crucify!"
Echoes their cry;
betrayed, mocked, and scourged,
Christ was sentenced to die.

The palms of His Hands
were bloodied and red;
a cruel crown of thorns
was pressed on His Head.

"Father, forgive them"
He cried from that tree;
"It is finished" at last!
His Love sets us free!

But Messiah, The King
defied death to its doom...

In silent triumph
He emerged from the tomb!

Seated in Glory
at the Father's right side,
He provides blessed rest;
sends His Spirit to guide.

So today, if *your* head
by shame is bowed down,
remember this phrase:
First the Cross;
Then the Crown!

1982

*John 19:5
**1 Corinthians 5:7b
℘

Love Psalm

Let's turn our thoughts toward the Awesome Presence of God. When in *Matthew 28:20*, Jesus told his disciples (and us, too), **"Lo, I am with you always,"** He meant in all places, in all circumstances, and at all times. We know this as The Omnipresence of God.

Yet, even when it seems that He is not in our present circumstances, He is there… "A friend who sticks closer than a brother," as in *Proverbs 18:24*. In *Hebrews 13:5*, Christ promised, **"I will never leave you or forsake you"** so that we may know that He will never withdraw His Presence or His help from us.

However, in order to sense His Presence, His nearness, and His dearness, we must first, "Be still and know that He is God." (*Psalm 46:10*)

In *1 Chronicles 16:11*, the writer tells us, "to Seek the Lord and His Strength; to seek His Presence continually." And *Hebrews 11:6* assures us that God is a rewarder of those who diligently seek Him.

James 4:8 urges us to "Draw near to God and He will draw near to us."

In *Isaiah 57:15* we find this Glorious Declaration: Thus says the High and Lofty one who inhabits Eternity, whose name is Holy, **"I dwell in the High and Holy place; with him, also, who has a humble and contrite spirit…to revive the spirit of the humble and the heart of the contrite ones."** These are the souls who are heart-broken because of their sin.

Here God reveals the secret of experiencing His Holy Presence: humility and repentance usher us into the Presence of Almighty God! Our tears of repentance are as precious jewels to Him.

He also inhabits the praises of His redeemed people, according to *Psalm 22:3*. That's why *Psalm 100* instructs us to "Come before His Presence with singing, to enter His gates with Thanksgiving, and into his courts with praise."

Because, Christianity is not a religion, but rather a *personal relationship* with our Beloved Savior, Jesus Christ, God's Holy Son, we have the sacred privilege of resting continually in His loving Presence, walking with Him, talking with Him…moment by moment, day-by-day. Here is how I discovered this Truth:

LOVE PSALM

I heard Messiah calling
"O Loved One, come away!"
He beckoned me with outstretched hand
to walk with Him that day.

When, failing to obey Him,
I waited for a sign,
He simply whispered winsome words:
"Dear Daughter, you are mine!"

With grateful heart, repentant,
I fell before my King;
His Gracious Hands were nail-rent
that from death Life may spring!

I found Him whom my soul does love;
I will not let Him go!
Beloved gift from Heav'n above
to sinners here below.

The perfume of His Presence…
that precious essence rare…
fills all my soul with singing,
and joy beyond compare!

1985

Behold The Lamb!

From time to time, I find it profitable to declare anew the reasons for my hope in the Lord Jesus Christ, my Savior, by reviewing some of the basic truths of the Gospel…His good news for all who would believe:

First and foremost is the familiar *John 3:16:* "For God so loved the world that he gave His only begotten Son, that whoever believes in Him should not perish, but have Everlasting life."

1 John 5:11, 12: "And this is the record that God has given to us Eternal Life, and this Life is in His Son. He who has the Son…has Life; He who does not have the Son of God, does not have Life."

Acts 4:12: "Neither is there salvation in any other, for there is no other name under Heaven given among men whereby we must be saved."

John 14:6 where Jesus says of Himself: **"I am the Way, the Truth, and The Life; no man comes to the Father except through me."**

Ephesians 2:8, 9: "For by Grace are you saved through Faith…and that not of yourselves: it is the gift of God…not of works, so that no one may boast."

John 10:10 where Jesus declares: **"I am come that they might have Life, and that they might have it more abundantly."**

And lastly…although there are many more such Scriptures, *John 1:29:* "Behold the Lamb of God who takes away the sin of the world!"

And Lo! A Voice from Heaven saying: **"This is my Beloved Son, in Whom I am well-pleased."** *Matthew 3:17*

These precious verses inspired these verses of mine:

Behold, The Lamb! *

He left behind His Glory,
He left behind His Throne;
Christ came below with men to dwell
and chose to call earth home.

His sinless Blood He gave
that sinful man may share
Redemption from the grave…
Deliverance through prayer.

He won my heart with Love,
He promised oil of Joy;
He told me that my Father's Love
no mortal can destroy.

I left behind my sorrow…
I left behind my pain…
I left behind my guilt and sin
with all its worldly stain.

He sent His Holy Spirit
when rising from the dead;
returning to His Glory,
He sent His Peace instead.

No sinner is too guilty,
no heart too filled with pain;
no life too torn or broken
for Him to mend again.

O Son of God, Most Holy,
You gave your life for me;
becoming meek and lowly…
your Love has set me free.

Today I long to serve Thee
for Thy Great Gift of Grace,
and urge the world to seek Thee
'til all behold Thy Face. Amen

February 22, 1981

* *John 1:29*

· 27 ·

CHRIST, THE LIFE!

I thank God for the privilege of sharing with you once again something He has laid on my heart. I'd like to comment on three little words that you've probably heard from your children, if you're a parent, or you may even have said them yourself. Those old familiar words, "It's not fair!"

Did you ever wonder where children get this sense of fairness and unfairness?

I believe that God has placed within each of us this awareness of justice and injustice, or fairness and unfairness, so that we may one day come to recognize what appears to be the most shameful case of injustice that the world has ever known: when the Holy, sinless Son of God became sin for us sinners and suffered our punishment, so that we, by repenting of sin and accepting His sacrifice, could be forgiven and stand clothed in Christ's righteousness before Almighty God. (*2 Corinthians 5:21*)

And in *2 Corinthians 8:9*, the Apostle Paul tells us that for our sakes Christ became poor: that is, He emptied Himself of His former Heavenly Glory, that through His poverty we might become rich in spiritual treasures and inherit Eternal Life with Him: Blessed be His Holy Name!

But *why* was Jesus willing to suffer and die in our place?

Because of these three wonderful words: *God Loves You* (and me, too!) as in *John 3:16*.

And because *God is Love*, and we are His special creation, He is not willing to let any of us perish in our sins.

There is no greater love than His!

As I studied this Sacred Sacrifice, and unfair exchange: His Death for our Eternal Life, the Lord graciously gave me these lines:

CHRIST, THE LIFE!

Because He drank the bitter cup,
I drink sweet cup of joy!
Because He drained its dregs of pain,
my cup is filled with health again;
to Christ all praise employ!

Because He carried crushing cross,
I need no longer bear my loss;
His comfort I enjoy!

Because He wore cruel crown of thorn,
I'll wear jeweled crown of souls reborn!
Because they nailed Him to a tree,
o'er sin I have the victory;
no more can guilt annoy!

Because He bled and died for me,
I am redeemed; He set me free,
and dread of death destroyed!

Because He was despised, ignored,
I am beloved, to God restored;
there is no greater joy!

Because He is alive today,
I bow my heart and humbly pray:
Lord Jesus, Savior, Prince of Peace,
Thy Love can make all evil cease;
O Resurrection and The Life,
come make an end of worldly strife! Amen.

February 21, 1979

John 11:25, 26
John 10:10

· 29 ·

Gospel Psalm

Although we are hearing a lot of bad news these days, we, as the family of God, can still rejoice as we recall the Good News:

The Glorious Gospel of our Lord and Savior Jesus Christ!

How it gladdens our hearts, as we bring to mind again the wond'rous words of *John 3:16*, that God so loved the world that he gave his only begotten Son, so that whoever believes in Him should not perish, but have Everlasting Life.

"And the Word was made flesh and dwelled among us, and we beheld His Glory—the Glory as of the only begotten of the Father, full of Grace and Truth," according to *John 1:14*.

In *John 10:10*, Jesus, the Messiah, declares, **"I am come that they might have Life and that they might have it more abundantly."**

Then in *John 14:6*, we hear Jesus announce, **"I am the Way, the Truth, and the Life; no one comes to the Father, except through me."**

In *John 11:25*, He further proclaims, **"I am the Resurrection and the Life; he who believes in me, 'though he may die, yet he shall live."**

And how often Christ tells us, **"Be of good cheer; fear not, nor be afraid."** When, in *John 14:1* He says, **"Let not your heart be troubled,"** we can look to our Holy Comforter with confidence and hope.

When in *Matthew 11:28* He calls, **"Come unto me all you who labor and are heavily-burdened, and I will give you rest,"** we can lean on His Everlasting Arms and find rest for our souls.

So, as we hide His Word in our hearts, we have a constant source of comfort during troubled times. By standing firmly on His precious promises, we can have His Peace in the midst of our storms.

And I, for one, need to remind myself of this Truth continually. To help me remember, the Lord gave me this little Gospel Psalm:

Gospel Psalm

Behold the crib, the cross, and the crown…
three Sacred symbols of Regal Renown.
To the crib Jesus came from above…
Gracious Gift of the Father's Great Love.

By His Blood on the cross He brought Peace…
to the prisoners of fear…sweet release…
to the troubled He spoke soothing calm…
to the suffering He applied healing balm.

Christ was willing to love-us-to-death,
and fill us with Hope and God's Holy Breath.
But he was despised and rejected by men,
and some would still dare to slay Him again.

But Death had no power to keep Christ enchained;
He escaped the grave and His Glory regained.
He'll return to reign crowned Victorious Lord,
forever revered, beloved, and adored!

"Even so come, Lord Jesus, Amen!"

December 16, 1987
Revised, 2002

EARTHEN VESSELS

There have been times in my life when I have felt like just a small smudge of dust on the face of the universe.

It was during those times that the Lord reminded me that, by His Grace, we have become the chosen children of our loving Heavenly Father through Jesus Christ, God's Holy Son, and our only Savior.

Because we believe that He shed His Holy Blood for our sins, we have received forgiveness, salvation, and Eternal Life, according to *Ephesians 1:3-7b*, and we are now "accepted in the Beloved." Blessed be His Holy Name!

Now, in *1 Corinthians, 1:26-31*, the writer states that not many wise, mighty, or noble people are called by God, but God has chosen the foolish things of the world to shame the wise. He has chosen the weak to shame the strong; he has chosen the lowly and despised and the things that are not, to nullify the things that are, so that no one may boast in His presence.

For what purpose did He choose us? The answer is found in *2 Corinthians 4:6,7*. He chose us so that the Light of the Glorious Gospel of Christ, which we have been given, should shine through us to a darkened and sinful world.

But we have this Gospel treasure in earthen vessels—these frail containers of clay, our mortal bodies, so that all Glory and Power may be attributed to God and not to us.

The Lord helped me to understand these Truths when He gave me this poem, which I call *Earthen Vessels*:

Earthen Vessels *

My spirit took an excursion today…
to Life's great display case
where in resplendent array
stood vessels of every description and size…
some worthy of note, to be praised and to prize.

There were vessels of onyx, of silver, of gold,
objects of beauty, a joy to behold;
vessels of valor, of honor, of fame,
but none of these vessels was graved with my name.

Then I beheld,
on the lowliest shelf,
a vessel of clay,
alone by itself.

It was battered and broken,
fragile and frail,
but its seams had been mended
in every detail.

I pondered, "What purpose has *this*
amidst all of *these*?"
The Potter, observing,
said, "Child, hear me please:

The gilded are lovely,
I have to agree,
but this one is special,
as soon you will see.

I love this poor vessel
'though it's shattered and *crazed*;

it is precious to me
'though its earthen, unglazed.

I am responsible for its design;
I fashioned it thus, because it is mine.
I saved it, by Grace, from destruction and loss;
with Blood was it purchased, so dear was its cost.
This vessel, now filled with my Spirit Divine,
reflects the bright glow of the Gospel Sublime.

Despise not this vessel,
nor put it to shame;
this vessel is *yours*, child;
it is scribed with your name!"

September 5, 1980

2 Corinthians 4:6,7

Occupied by The Lord:
A Carpenter's Consecration

An important question for all of us is, "What does the Lord require of believers?" God Himself gives us the answer through the Prophet *Micah 6:8*.

What does the Lord require of you? "To do justly, to love mercy, and to walk humbly, with your God." We need only to consider the last part, because if we walk humbly with our God, I believe that we will also be just and merciful. Amen!

But *how* do we walk humbly with our God? And what is humility, really? The Scriptures tell us to be *clothed with humility* (*1 Peter 5:5*), and to humble ourselves as a little child (*Matthew 18:4*).

It's a strange thing about humility—the moment you might think you *have* it, you've *lost* it. So how could anyone boast of being humble? But, to our God, humility is a precious jewel, having many facets, and is called by some, *the vessel of all graces*.

It gleams in faithful obedience, as when Abram answered God's call to leave his idolatrous nation and to go to an unknown land (*Genesis 12:1-3*).

Another *facet* is submission to God's will as in *Luke 1:38*, when Mary, chosen to bear the Messiah, told the Angel Gabriel, "Let it be to me according to Thy word."

It is also *reflected* by Christ in the Garden of Gesthemene, when He prayed: **"Oh my Father, if it is possible, let this cup pass from me; nevertheless, not as I will, but as You will."** (*Mathew 26:39*)

Humility is clearly evident in repentance of sin, as demonstrated by the publican who cried, "God be merciful to me, a sinner!" (*Luke 18:13*)

In the next verse, Jesus declares, **"Everyone who exalts himself shall be abased and he who humbles himself shall be exalted."** So that we may know that Humility is the opposite of pride, a sin which God despises.

Humility is also displayed when a person bears the insults and injustice of another without retaliating, as Jesus exemplified in *1 Peter 2:23*: "When He was reviled, or cruelly treated, he did not return insult for insult; when he suffered, He did not threaten."

It also takes Humility to endure suffering and misfortune with Grace, as did the Apostle Paul, who sang God's Praise even while imprisoned, and when his prayer for healing was denied. He accepted the thorn in his flesh, so that the Power of Christ would rest upon him. (*2 Corinthians 12:7-9*) In *Galatians 6:14* he vows, "God forbid that I should glory, but in the Cross of Jesus Christ."

There are many more such beautiful examples of Humility in the Bible, to be sure, but it still shines today in worship, in a thankful heart, in forgiveness, in sacrifice, and in willingness to work and witness for love of our Lord.

Our Gracious Lord has given me this devotional prayer as an illustration of simple humility:

Occupied By The Lord
(A Carpenter's Consecration)

Lord, while you traversed this earth
you worked at this same ordinary occupation…

Today, this rough-hewn board before me
seems symbolic of my coarse, unfinished life
in your hands.

At this very moment you are busy
creating a useful object
from the flawed lumber of my life.

I pray that I shall not become warped
as daily I am exposed to the harsh elements
of this world.

I know it will require much planing and filing
to smooth away the rough corners of my character.

Although at times you have had to use
the hammer of adversity
to pound some sense into me,
I pray that I shall never crack and become useless
from those beneficial blows.

These nails, Lord, serve as constant reminder
of those that pierced your Precious Palms;
You bore those wounds gladly for my sake,
and I thank you for your selfless sacrifice.

Please use *my* calloused hands, Lord,
to do Thy work in the world;
and may I ever measure up
to your requirements of me. Amen.

December 10, 1975

FOR THE PRIZE

All of you probably know that the Bible compares The Christian Life to a foot race. In the Book of *Hebrews 12:1*, it is written, "…let us run with patience the race that is set before us."

In *Philippians 3:13, 14*, the Apostle *Paul* encourages himself, and us, with these words: "…this one thing I do: forgetting those things which are behind, and reaching forth unto those things which are before (us), I press toward the mark for the prize of the high calling of God in Christ Jesus."

The Lord used these scripture to inspire me to write this little poem, called *For the Prize*. May it encourage your heart today.

For the Prize *

We're running a Race…
we cannot quit now;
we're leaving this place…
we've taken a vow!

'Though slow to begin,
we're picking up speed;
there's Heaven to win…
and Christ in the lead!

We dare not look back…
nor left…nor right;
our feet right on track,
we'll press on with might!

While striving ahead
with eyes on our goal,
God's Spirit has fed
and quickened our soul.

When the pathway turns rough,
and our courage is gone,
He'll provide strength enough…
if we *keep keeping on.*

'Though the course may seem long,
we'll triumph, by Grace,
and we'll sing Victory's Song
in that Glorious Place! Amen!

November 14, 1985

Hebrews 12:1
Philippians 3:13,14

જી

Night Song

Because God is Gracious, our nation will once again celebrate Thanksgiving Day during this coming week.

But we, as the children of our loving Heavenly Father, know that *every* day is Thanksgiving Day—not only because of His bountiful Goodness to us, but also for Who He Is; Our Blessed Lord and Savior!

In Christ, He has given us the precious gift of His Forgiveness and His Love, Joy, Peace, Freedom, Fellowship, Hope, and Eternal Life!

"Thanks be to God for His indescribable Gift!" (*2 Corinthians 9:15*) All He asks of us in return is a grateful and obedient heart. God takes great delight in an attitude of gratitude, as the Scriptures instruct us:

Psalm 107:1,2, "Oh give thanks unto the Lord, for He is good, because His mercy endures forever. Let the redeemed of the Lord say so, whom He has redeemed from the hand of the enemy."

Psalm 95:2, "Let us come before His Presence with Thanksgiving, and make a joyful noise unto Him with psalms."

Psalm 100:4, "Enter into His gates with Thanksgiving and into His courts with Praise; be thankful unto Him and Bless His name."

1 Thessalonians 5:18, "In everything give thanks, for this is the will of God, in Christ Jesus, concerning you."

And even when we don't feel like it, "let us sacrifice the sacrifices of Thanksgiving and declare his works with rejoicing." (*Psalm 107:22*)

And also *Ephesians 5:20*, "Giving thanks always for all things unto God the Father, in the name of the Lord Jesus Christ."

And now, *Revelation 7:12*, "Blessing and Glory and Wisdom and Thanksgiving and Honor and Power and Might be unto our God forever and ever, Amen!"

Although I could never thank Him adequately, the Lord once gave me this little poem with which to praise Him:

Night Song

Maker-of-moonbeams,
Shaper-of-stars,
Painter-of-rainbows,
How Wond'rous You are!

Keeper-of-sparrows,
Healer-of-hearts,
Father, your children
love Who You Are!

O Saver-of-souls,
soon-coming King,
Lord God of Glory,
Your Praises we sing!

March 5, 1990

My Going-On Song

We all know that, as the family of God, we are called to encourage others, as we are given the opportunity. Yet, there are times in each of our lives when we must also encourage ourselves and to be encouraged *by* others.

Even the great saints of old found this to be so, and they left us many precious verses of encouragement, such as *Psalm 27:1*, where David, the Psalmist, declares, "The Lord is my Light and my Salvation, whom shall I fear? The Lord is the strength of my life, of whom shall I be afraid?"

We're all familiar with the beautiful *23rd Psalm*, which has comforted countless numbers of heavy hearts.

In *Psalm 103*, David commands his soul to Bless the Lord for all His benefits: His Forgiveness, Healing, Deliverance, Provision, Renewal, His Loving-Kindness and Tender Mercies.

In *Psalm 34:8*, David affirms, "O taste and see that the Lord is Good!"

In *Psalm 94:19*, we find this precious gem: "In the multitude of my thoughts within me, Thy Comforts delight my soul!"

In *Nahum 1:7*, the Prophet proclaims, "The Lord is Good; a stronghold in the day of trouble, and He knows those who trust in Him."

God Himself comforts *Joshua* in *1:9*, **"Be strong and of good courage; be not afraid, for the Lord your God is with you wherever you go."**

Isaiah in *40:31* declares, "They that wait upon the Lord shall renew their strength."

In *Romans 8:31*, the Apostle Paul asks, "If God be for us, who can be against us?"

In *Philippians 4:13*, Paul professes: "I can do all things through Christ who strengthens me!"

Nehemiah in *8:10* agrees, "The joy of the Lord is your strength!"

Jesus comforts His Disciples in the *Gospel of John 14:1*, **"Let not your heart be troubled!"** And again in *14:27*, **"Peace I leave with you."**

"Therefore, my beloved brothers, be steadfast, unmoveable, always abounding in the work of the Lord, because you know that your labor is not in vain in the Lord!" (*1 Corinthians 15:58*)

Galatians 6:9 says, "Let us not be weary in well-doing, for in due time we shall reap results if we do not give up!"

I praise God for these, and many more such inspiring Scriptures. I thank Him for also giving me my little *Going-On Song*:

My Going-On Song

I belong to *The One* Who loves us most;
I've been bought by The Blood of The Lamb…
kept by the Power of The Holy Ghost,
I'm secure in my Father's Right Hand!

I'm walking with Christ in the narrow way…
guided step-by-step by His Hand…
onward and upward day-by-day
'til I enter His Beautiful Land! Amen!

August 31, 1991

STAYED!

Today let's think about…thoughts! First, let's consider God's thoughts toward us:

In *Isaiah 55:8,9*, God declares that His thoughts and ways are higher than our thoughts and ways. And so they are.

But *Jeremiah 29:11* assures us that God's thoughts toward us are those of Peace and not of evil, to give us a future and a hope.

In *Psalm 139:17*, David, the Psalmist, exclaims, "How precious are your thoughts to me, O God!"

Now, what about *our* thoughts toward God, toward others, and toward the circumstances of our lives?

Hebrews 4:12 tells us that God knows our very thoughts and even our motives. What a sobering thought that is!

So how can we control our thought-life to make it pleasing to our Holy God? The mind has been compared to a battleground where a constant struggle rages between our positive, good, and Godly thoughts and our negative, worldly, and unholy thoughts.

You may ask, "How can we hope to win this mental battle?" Here is our answer: By putting on the spiritual armor of God, as described in *Ephesians 6:10-17*, and by using the sword of the Lord, the mighty Word of God!

Because "the weapons of our warfare are not carnal, but mighty through God, to the pulling down of strongholds; casting down imaginations and every high thing that exalts itself against the knowledge of God."

Verses 4 and 5 of *2 Corinthians Chapter 10* further tell us to bring every thought captive to the obedience of Christ (I'm still working on that!)

Because we know that to be carnally-minded is death and is enmity toward God, but to be spiritually-minded is life and peace, according to *Romans 8:6, 7*.

So, whatever things are True, Noble, Just, Pure, Lovely, of Good Report, Virtuous, or Praiseworthy, let us think on these things, as in *Philippians 4:8*.

There is an especially lovely verse that helps to draw my wandering mind back to God. It's found in *Psalms 94:19*, "In the multitude of my thoughts within me, thy comforts delight my soul!"

And *Isaiah 26:3,4* gives us the precious promise that God will keep us in perfect peace if our minds are stayed on Him, because we trust in Him. The Lord gave me a little poem based on these verses to show us how we can live continually in His Presence and in His Peace:

STAYED! *

O, the mind that is stayed
shall not be afraid
when stayed on The Father above.

The mind kept unswayed
receives comfort and aid…
Precious Gifts of God's Gracious Love.

A Faith that's secure
can survive and endure
any trial and not be dismayed.

Despite every test,
Perfect Peace, Perfect Rest
belong to the mind that is stayed.

If Hope stays unshaken,
and doubts are forsaken…
what matter if plans be delayed?

Christ's Joy is still ours
just for the taking,
but consider the price Jesus paid!

For staying the mind,
my friends, you will find
there is really only one way:

When troubles assail us,
God's Peace will not fail us
if we'll trust in His Love as we pray!

October 16, 1979

*Isaiah 26:3

· 45 ·

REFRESHING

It's summer, so let's talk about R&R, God's kind of R&R, Renewal and Refreshing in Him!

How often the Word of God invites us to rest in the Lord as in *Psalms 37:7*. This means to be silent to the Lord, avoiding all complaints, anger, and hasty actions.

Zepheniah 1:7 also tells us to be silent in the presence of the Lord, during difficult times, because silence can calm a troubled heart.

Jeremiah 6:16 urges us to "Ask where the good way is and to walk in it; then we will find rest for our souls."

Ephesians 4:22, 23, instructs us to forsake the old ungodly life and be renewed in the spirit of our minds.

2 Corinthians 4:16 is a precious promise to senior saints, "Do not lose heart, even though our outward man is perishing, yet the inward man is being renewed day-by-day."

David, in his well-loved *23rd Psalm*, declares that he is led beside the still waters where God restores his soul.

Isaiah 40:31 reminds us that those who wait upon the Lord shall have their strength renewed.

In *Isaiah 30:15*, God affirms that in quietness and confidence shall be our strength.

In *Matthew 11:28*, Jesus Himself invites us to come to Him and find rest for our souls.

God calls us always to abide in His Word and in His Will, because, "This is the rest by which He causes the weary to rest and this is the Refreshing!"

This beautiful verse, *Isaiah 28:12*, inspired this poem:

REFRESHING *

Verdant splendor, russet mountains
thrusting peaks above the plain;
rushing streams and gushing fountains;
God speaks Beauty once again!

And this is refreshing.

Indian paintbrush lace the tundra,
blend their blush with blossoms blue;
here I pause to gaze in wonder
at a canvas ever new.

And this is refreshing.

Purple finches trill their anthems
'til my heart with rapture wells;
azure skies guide eyes toward Heaven
where the Master Artist dwells.

Yes, this is refreshing.

But heart at rest, with Christ's enmeshing…
cool contentment, quiet calm;
gift of God's most precious blessing
in His Peace, the soul's sweet balm.

And this is *the* Refreshing!

April 27, 1990

*Isaiah 28:12
*Hebrews 4:9-11

ℰᴐ

INVITATION

Since June is the month of love, weddings, brides, and bridegrooms, it seems fitting today to recall a few Scriptures that describe the Church as the Bride of Christ, the dearly loved wife of our Heavenly *Bridegroom* Jesus!

Because God Is Love, as in *1 John 4:8* and *16*, He reveals to us, by the example of bride and groom, that our relationship to Him should be so dear, so tender and affectionate, that we would long to live near to His heart of Love always and forever, Amen!

In the Gospel of *Matthew, Chapter 25*, we read the Parable of the 10 bridesmaids. In verse 6, a shout is heard, "The Bridegroom is coming, go out to meet Him." Now the five wise young ladies were prepared to meet the bridegroom, and to accompany Him to the wedding feast, but the five unwise were not fully prepared, were not allowed to attend the festivities, and were left behind.

Because Christ said that He is coming again, we, too, are awaiting His arrival at any time. This precious promise, is found in *John 14:2, 3*, Jesus said, **"I go to prepare a place for you and I will come again and receive you unto myself, that where I am, there you may be also."**

Matthew 25:13 tells us to watch, because we don't know the day or hour when Jesus will come back for us.

1 Thessalonians 5:2 affirms that the Lord will come for believers unexpectedly…"as a thief in the night."

In *Revelation 22:12 and 22:20*, Jesus Himself declares, **"Behold I come quickly!"**

Additional advance notice of Christ's coming for us in His Glory is found in *Matthew 16:27, Matthew 25:31, Luke 21:27*, and several other Scriptures. Now when the Lord returns, He will find only two kinds of believers: those who are ready to meet him, and sadly, those who are *not*.

Revelation 19:7-9, describes His arrival, "Let us be glad and rejoice and give Him Glory, for the marriage supper of the Lamb has come and His wife has made herself ready. And to her it was granted to be dressed in fine linen, clean and bright, for the fine linen is the righteous acts of the saints"—and that's what He calls *us*.

Then in *verse 9* the Angel said to the Apostle John, "Write, *Blessed are those who are called to the marriage supper of the Lamb!*" and these are the true sayings of God.

Our Gracious Lord sent me this engraved invitation based on these verses in *Revelation 19*:

INVITATION *

Are you ready for the Wedding?
Are you wearing Righteous White?
Have you read The Grand Announcement?
Christ is coming for His Bride!

With this Joyous Proclamation
Heaven's Bells will soon resound;
at this Sacred Celebration
Angel Anthems will abound.

Have you met The Blessed Bridegroom?
How He loves The Church, His *Wife*!
Jesus paid the debt of dowry
when He Bled to save her life!

How should we await His coming?
Pledge to Him our Reverent Vow;
daily seek Him at The Altar;
Love Him! Praise Him! Serve Him now!

June 15, 1984

Revelation 19:7-9

ℰ

HEAVENLY HOPE

Let's take another look at something that's invisible, but nearly as necessary to our lives as the air we breathe.

After we have received all the necessities and blessings of life: food, clothing, shelter, and even love, we still need something more to enable us to live an overcoming and victorious life.

When life's difficulties, disappointments, illnesses, and problems come against us, we will also need a steadfast *hope* to get us through those trials.

Hebrews 11:1 tells us that, "Faith is the substance of things *hoped*-for, the evidence of things not seen."

In *Romans 8:24, 25*, the Apostle Paul writes, "We are saved in this Hope; but Hope that is *seen* is not Hope, because why does one still hope for what he sees? But if we hope for that which we do *not* see, then we will wait for it with perseverance."

And for *what* are we waiting? First of all, we look to God to provide the strength and courage to endure our desperate circumstances. Perhaps we await the solution of a difficult problem, or a healing, or the salvation of loved ones. It's all about *not giving up*; it's about clinging to Hope even when things seem hopeless.

In *Psalm 31:24*, David, the Psalmist, declares, "Be of good courage and He shall strengthen your heart, all you who hope in The Lord."

In *Psalm 146:5*, David says, "Happy is he whose Hope is in The Lord!"

In *Psalm 147:11*, He tells us that The Lord takes pleasure in those who hope in His Mercy.

Now, sad to say, sometimes the answer to our prayers does not come during our lifetime, as when Paul prayed three times for the thorn in his flesh to be removed; still it remained.

That's when God, in *2 Corinthians 12:9* said to Paul, and to us, too, **"My Grace is sufficient for you, for my strength is made perfect in weakness."** This means that our infirmities are God's opportunity to show forth His Power through our submission to His Will.

So in *Romans 8:18*, Paul concludes that, "The sufferings of this present time are not worthy to be compared with the Glory which shall be revealed in us." Praise God, in Christ we also have Hope of Eternal Life!

In the *Gospel of John, 14:1*, Jesus comforts us with these familiar words, **"Let not your heart be troubled, I go to prepare a place for you, and I will come again and take you to myself that where I Am there you may be also."**

This is my *Heavenly Hope*:

HEAVENLY HOPE*

I do not ask that mansions fair
should be prepared for me on high;
array, I pray, some haven where
no care could cause my soul to sigh.

I do not seek some priceless prize
or comely crown to grace my head;
just let me see Messiah's eyes
smile kindly into mine, instead.

All that awaits us over there
of purest pleasure, endless bliss...
shall not be worthy to compare
with such a Glorious sight as this:

When finally my life is past,
and I arise to flee earth's harms...
arriving safely Home, at last,
I'm gathered to my Savior's Arms!

September 6, 1984

* *John 14:1-3*

·51·

...AND OTHER POEMS

ETERNAL DAWN

Man wakes to Life as morn to dazzling dawn;
Bright with eternal hope of radiant day…
Warmed by the sun of laughter he is drawn
To cry for time to grant his dreams display.
His eye discerns approaching sky of night;
Mysterious stillness of that somber shade
That etches on his soul the secret fright
Of nameless terrors that make man afraid.
Watching the waste of westward-waning sun,
Bemoaning the brute brevity of Life…
Pondering the tasks he's left undone…
He counts for naught his purpose and his strife;

  Yet echo of Eternal Life, on earth,
  Glows in the promise of each dawn's rebirth.

  1961

Just as a craftsman polishes ordinary stone to a high lustre to produce an object of beauty, so is God portrayed in this sonnet as The Great Artificer Who ennobles the soul of man through His instruments: Pain and Suffering...

CELESTIAL LAPIDARY

God embellishes man's soul with sorrow;
abrasive pain the wheel on which it's ground.
Learnéd Lapidary, He may borrow
imperfect stones such as on earth abound.
When cruel the brutal blows we suffer,
'though we bewail our fate and cry *unjust*!
rough adversity serves as His buffer;
our tears compound the oil for diamond dust.
Acute afflictions, although acrid acids,
their Celestial spectral lights reflect
like diamonds of a million brilliant facets
suffusing some translucent blue effect.

Dare mortal man The Hand of God condemn
that carves his soul to form a precious gem?

1961

FEAR THE MASTER!

Beneath the pharoah-whip of fear man cowers,
Crouching as to elude his unknown foes.
Enslaved by cruel despotic powers;
Dismayed by vague restraining chains, he goes
His trembling way through ineffectual life,
Blaming on dreaded perils that bear threat
His lack of manly courage to face strife;
Cursing the fates-that-be when trials beset
Him; lashed by dark doubts, his timorous qualm
Serves but to tighten fear's confining chain,
Preventing solace and escape to calm;
Inflicting further lacerating pain.

       To loose the shackles that bind soul to fear,
       Obeisance to one God man must revere.

1961

BRIGHT PROMISE

Once these Great Glorious Words were spoken:
"Lo, I have set my bow within the cloud." *
Heralding a promise never broken…
By Almighty God these words were vowed:
"My covenant with you will I remember…
Witness my rainbow in the darkened sky!"
Rich hues suffusing vivid splendor
Bear proof each raging storm shall pass you by.
By foaming flood I'll ne'er destroy this Earth…
Though once the wicked I engulfed this way.
So dedicate your life to me for worth
That all your fearsome storms I may allay.

> Each rainbow speaks anew His Vow Divine;
> Pledge Him, in turn, to make your life sublime.

1961

Genesis 9:16

BREAD *

Love is the bread for which I yearn and strive!
One slice will not suffice to quell my dream.
I crave a loaf to keep my soul alive;
Such rich repast is not in Nature's scheme.
My hungry heart recalls the barren field
Where much is sown, yet there is naught to reap.
'Though planting love, I glean no golden yield.
My loveless life, like Earth in fallow sleep,
Awaits a joyous rain to sate its thirst;
Cool nectar to revive like verdant Spring,
And cause a precious seed to swell and burst
With eagerness its nourishment to bring.

> Sweet grain, in arid soil, returns to dust;
> While I, unloved, still hunger for a crust.

1961

* John 6:35

SERENITY

Once I was
        a restless ocean-of-a-woman,
                ever seeking fascinating shores.

I set my heart adrift
        'midst crashing currents,
           braving the brute billows
                that broke my hope
                    against the rugged reefs
                        of Disappointment and Despair;
                            engulfed in waves of salty tears
                                    was I.

Emerging as from chasmal deep,
        eyeing the silent shores of Loneliness,
                I came to rest upon a shadowed shoal
                        and slept.

Waking afresh,
        I felt God's Hand upon my heart.
           "Trust!" was the only word
                He spoke.

The turbulency ebbed about me;
        cool, tranquil waters bore me up
                in silence
                    and repose.

1965

MANGER MUSINGS *

This is the news the prophets bring;
this is the song the angels sing:
'A helpless babe shall be called King!'

The mind of God conceived Love's Plan
whereby His Spirit became man;
Messiah-in-a-swaddling cloth
against whom hostile men were wroth.

Who would have thought that tender babe,
so gently in the manger laid,
would one day have to die for me
that I might live eternally?

Who would believe that infant sweet
would needs be bruised from head to feet?
Who would have thought that tiny hand
would shed its blood on Israel's sand?
Who could have guessed that precious head
would bear *my* shame and curse instead?

The sin that severed man from God...
and kept him bound to earth's dread sod...
was laid on Christ at Calvary
that by His death we'd be set free!

Who would believe He lives again
to cleanse and comfort sin-sick men?
Who would believe this mystery?
Lord, *I* believe your Word, Amen!

December 13, 1980

Isaiah 9:6,7 and Isaiah 53

And We Beheld His Glory!

Let's recall those beloved, familiar words of *Isaiah*, the prophet, in *Chapter 9:6*.

"For unto us a child is born, unto us a Son is given; and the government shall be upon His shoulder; and His Name shall be called Wonderful, Counselor, the Mighty God, the Everlasting Father, the Prince of Peace."

We also remember these glorious verses from the book of *John 1:1* and *14*:

"In the beginning was The Word, and The Word was *with* God, and the Word *was* God."

"And The Word was made flesh and dwelt among us, and we beheld His Glory, the Glory as of the only begotten of The Father, full of Grace and Truth." I Bless His Holy Name!

Some time ago, the Lord gave me this poem to help me to better understand the coming of Messiah Jesus to earth. I call it *And We Beheld His Glory*!

And We Beheld His Glory! *

In manger-cradled Majesty…
enwrapped in humble infancy…
Messiah came to set us free!
And We Beheld His Glory!

Embodied Grace and Truth was He…
Whose Righteousness and Charity
restored lost man to dignity;
O What a Glorious Story!

When Holy Hands by nails were scarred…
Our Savior's Face by suffering marred…
the cursing crowd paid no regard
when darkness veiled His Glory.

But when that evil deed was done,
Eternal Life had just begun,
and vict'ry over death was won;
From Calvary Came Glory!

He's coming soon as King to reign;
our waiting shall not be in vain;
we'll praise our Lord with this refrain:
Behold the King of Glory! Amen!

December 21, 1986

*John 1:14

ℱᴀ

THE STILL, SMALL VOICE *

You cannot still The Still, Small Voice
that draws you to The Savior!
God calls: *Come make My Son your choice;*
forsake your bold behavior!

You've tried to drown The Sacred Sound
by pleasure or by labor…
but nowhere else can Peace be found
than in God's Loving Favor.

Christ's Gracious Gift you dare not spurn
that purchased your Salvation;
this Gift…good deeds could never earn…
will keep you from temptation.

The Blood-Stained Cross is whispering still
to every listening soul:
Come, kneel and yield your heart and will;
Christ's Love will make you whole!

January 2, 1997

1 Kings 19:12
Jeremiah 31:3
Matthew 11:28-29
Psalm 46:10

DEVOTION

Breath-of-my-Life,
I long for Thy filling!
Spirit Sublime,
my whole heart is willing.
O send down the Peace
that descends like a Dove;
still me, then fill me
with Thy Tender Love.

Tender Love…
Tender Love…
still me,
then fill me
with Thy Tender Love. Amen.

August 6, 1983

FRUITION *

Thou Art The Mighty Vine, Lord Jesus,
while I am but a tiny twig
of whom you desire much fruit;
without You, Lord, I can do nothing!

You are The Source of Life-Giving Water
and the Steadfast Sonlight
essential for its growth.

How often this branch has been purged
that I might bring forth ever more fruit!
Yet, despite the pangs of Thy cutting knife
on my life,
I have abided in Thee, by Thy Grace.

Although my yield is still small, Lord,
may its sweetness increase by Thy Favor,
so that hungering souls may savor
the Fragrant Fruit of Thy Love. Amen.

February 17, 1979

John 15:5
Galatians 5:22

THE LESSON *

Christ's disciples vied for position
at Messiah's Mighty Throne...
but He, disdaining ambition,
made His displeasure known.

Divesting Himself of His Glory,
in servant's garb attired,
He illustrated His story
with intention to inspire.

Before His listeners bending
in sweet humility,
He exhibited Love Unending
for flawed humanity.

When Peter voiced strong objection:
"You'll never wash *my* feet!"
Christ countered with kind correction:
"Your cleansing is not complete!"

Next He bathed the feet of Judas,
aware that he'd betray
The Son of God, our Savior,
that dark and dreadful day.

Here's the object of that day's lesson
taught in the Master's 'school':
To make our lives on earth a blessing
we must learn to *serve*, not to *rule*!

June 6, 1996

John 13:1-20
Matthew 23:11, 12

A Knitter's Prayer

Lord, as I design this…
the afghan-of-my-Life…
my gift to Thee…
may the quality of its fabric
be of cheerful and harmonious hue;
may its texture remain clean, soft and yielding
to Thy touch;

may its interlocking stitches
symbolize Thy children
with whom I interact each day;
may we be knit ever more inseparably together
to form a pleasing pattern in Thy sight;

may I not be ashamed to reveal
the concealed side of my work;
let there be no unsightly knots
or ugly tangles there;
and if I should make an error,
please help me to unravel my mistake
and to proceed anew,
although it be a tedious and difficult task.

When it is finished, Lord,
may the afghan-of-my-Life
spread warmth and comfort
over all whom it touches, Amen.

February 12, 1972

The Sweet of Soul

Imprisoned in imperfect bodies,
Some, graceless, deformed;
Helpless, love-starved souls
Craving acceptance
Enduring rejection;
Nature's incomplete clay,
Limited by stunted minds,
Shunned, mocked, tormented,
Inarticulate…bewildered.
      These are the sweet of soul;
      These are the warm of heart;
      They know nothing of malice,
      Nothing of greed.
      How they respond
      To an endearing word!
      How their faces light
      At a smile!
      What warmth emanates
      From their timid touch!
      Their souls, thank God,
      Are perfectly whole!

1963

HELEN KELLER—A TRIBUTE

Child of the ceaseless silence;
child of incessant night;
denied the light of life…
inspired others…smiling!

We, foolish mortals,
who can see and hear
the waves upon the shore,
dread death…
when we shall see
and hear no more.

She, who ne'er saw sun,
nor rainbow radiant
in the sky
must dwell now in delight
within that place
where she beholds, at last,
the Greatest Light of all:
God's Holy Face!

July 11, 1968

OUTCRY!

America, O Lovely Land,
cursed be the stains upon thine hand;
your garments smirched with crimson red
by blood of innocents you've shed!

'Though tiny bodies writhe with pain,
you hide your eyes; they strive in vain.
Their little lips form soundless cry:
"What is our crime, that we must die?"

These miracles in mothers' wombs
are scraped and suctioned into tombs;
these victims of the careless throng
shall never hear the lark's sweet song;

nor ever see a blossom's blush,
nor feel the twilight's blessed hush.
They shall not wonder at a star,
nor probe its mysteries afar.

These precious visitors to earth,
immortal souls *before* their birth,
by heartless men are being slain;
while they, for murder, garner gain.

Awake America; Repent!
For judgment is The Lord's intent.
Almighty God is speaking still:
"All life is mine; thou shalt not kill!"

July 3, 1983

CONSOLATION *

"You shall not always weep, my Child,
you shall not always weep;
one day your darkness will be light
I my promise keep."

Thus spoke my Lord to me one day,
amidst my deepest gloom,
while on my face in tears I lay
within my lonely room.

"Just for a night shall weeping last;
your joy, like morning sun,
dawns fair…the darkness soon is past;
new life has just begun!"

Once more I dried my fallen tears
on hearing this refrain;
His words erased my foolish fears
and I could smile again.

"Take heart, my child, and weep no more…"
I heard my Savior croon;
"Look up, my child, the night is o'er;
I'm coming for you soon!"

Even so come, Lord Jesus. Amen.

May 29, 1981

* *Psalm 30:5*

Before I Go Home

Dear Lord, my heart's desire impart to me
before I go to be with Thee:
I long to see loved souls set free
before I go Home.

From darkness to Thy Light at last…
out of the sadness of the past…
with Loving Kindness seal them fast
before I go Home.

May they be with Thy Spirit filled…
covered by The Blood you spilled…
let every doubt and fear be stilled
before I go Home.

Grant, Gracious Lord, my last request:
That they would by Thy Peace be blessed…
so that my heart may be at rest
before I go Home. Amen.

July 12, 1991

MY SONG *

He turned my mourning
into dancing,
and girded me with gladness;
He broke the chains of sadness
and cast them all away!

My heart is now rejoicing;
my mouth is filled with laughter…
His Spirit keeps me singing
all along Life's way!

He turned my mourning
into dancing,
and girded me with gladness…
my song shall praise His Glory
forever and a day!

August 26, 1983

Psalms 30:11,12

ENIGMA

What purpose should this vessel serve?
Why did the craftsman so conceive
its quaint design?
Why did he fashion jasper jar in sage?
Why laced he it with tracery so fine?

How frail it is! Imperiled by a careless blow,
and yet its subtle symmetry
deserves display
to grace some barren space.

How fragile, too, this woman's heart;
how vulnerable to slightest blow;
why did the Master Craftsman
deign to shape it so?

In this harsh age
we've need of metal vessels…shatterproof;
and hearts impervious to pain.
But then, what tender touch of beauty
could their durability contain?

May 9, 1970

MESSIAH'S SONG

Said Jesus:
Sufficient for thee is My Grace
your sin and your guilt to erase.
Life Eternal is free
for believing in Me;
My Grace is sufficient for thee! *

In each sorrow or burden you bear
My Rest and Sweet Comfort I'd share;
cast your care upon me, **
Seek My Peace and you'll see
My Grace is sufficient for thee!

Says The Lord to each struggling saint:
Men ought always to pray and not faint; ***
when you long to give up
come partake of this cup:
My Grace is sufficient for thee!

His Grace is sufficient for *me*
whatever my trial may be.
When Life's Journey seems long,
my soul echoes this song:
Thy Grace is sufficient for me!

October 7, 1987

2 Corinthians 12:9
** *1 Peter 5:7*
*** *Luke 18:1*

WORDS FOR THE WOUNDED

God will not crush the feeble reed,
nor quench the smoldering flax; *
His Grace and Strength are all we need
to quell our foe's attacks.

Within His Word God makes it clear
that we must bear our grief
with spirit sweet, not craven fear,
'til He provides relief.

In Nature's realm we see displayed
our Maker's quaint concern;
by each creation is portrayed
some lesson we may learn.

God does not split the chrysalis
to free the butterfly;
its struggle must precede its bliss
when wings take to the sky.

The oyster strains against sand's grain
that irritates his skin,
producing precious pearls from pain…
His gift divine within.

The willow sighs, yet is not weak;
by weeping is made strong…
Dear Friend, I know whereof I speak
from weeping came this song!

January 10, 1995

Isaiah 42:3

ॐ

LOVE LINES

Lord, may I daily walk with Thee,
by Grace, in *Thine* integrity!

Daily mankind is put to this test…
to relinquish the thing that his heart loves the best.
But God gives us His *Truth* to know in its place…
and His Light reflects best from a tear-glistened face.

Nothing is too difficult for Thee
For Thou Art The God Who healeth me!

Behold His Holiness
All people of the earth!
Come now in lowliness;
declare Messiah's Worth!

We would have perished long ago
had You not cared and loved us so!

Just a few more weary days and then
Jesus is coming again!

What would I do without Jesus?
What would I do without Him?
I'd still be lost in gross darkness—
I'd still be steeped in my sin.

Where would I be without Jesus?
I'd still be wandering alone—
If I had not yielded to Jesus
and bowed at His Merciful Throne.

I took an exodus from sorrow,
I left it all behind;
my eyes are fixed upon tomorrow
while Christ renews my mind.

This moment *Now*
is all we own
of Life on earth
'ere it has flown.

We need not despair…
We're safe in His care!

Lord, by Thy Merciful Hand
Let there be Peace in our Land!

Waiting on The Lord
Brings great reward.

The sacred, secret path of sorrow
leads to promised joys tomorrow.

Sar Shalom, Prince of Peace,
May Thy Mercies never cease!

I plead the Blood of The Lamb
over our sin-sickened Land.

Nothing of this world avails…
Nothing in this world prevails…
Our lives are all futility
apart from Thee, O Lord; apart from Thee!

When I grow weary, so weary I'm falling,
then I hear Jesus, my Sweet Savior calling:

"Be a little stronger, just a little longer;
Come, Child, I'll hold you, comfort, enfold you…
tenderly guide you, walk right beside you…
My Father loves you! Father loves you!"

I did not know that Jesus loves me;
I did not know He really cares;
I did not know He died to save me;
I did not know He answers prayers.

He sent a friend to show forth kindness;
to demonstrate His Love aright;
He sent His Light to end my blindness:
His radiant Face dispelled the night!

Thy Love alone, O Lord...
Thy Love alone...
can heal the wounded heart
and melt the heart of stone.

Thy Love alone, O Lord,
Thy Love alone...
can save an empty life
and fill it with Thine Own!

I fell in love with Jesus
when I read His Gentle Word;
His was the sweetest message
my heart had ever heard.

O God of Eternity,
just let us be
forever together
in Glory with Thee!

ABOUT THE AUTHOR

Lee Bain Chiaro relates her journey from orphaned Holocaust victim to victorious Christian through poetry. Her tract, *Forbidden Quest*, describes the experiences that led to her life-changing decision. Today she shares her testimony, Scriptural teachings, and poetry readings in Colorado, where she lives with her husband and grown family.

Forbidden Quest is available through The Gospel Tract Society, P.O. Box 1118, Independence, Missouri, 64051-9988.

0-595-25611-2

www.ingramcontent.com/pod-product-compliance
Lightning Source LLC
Chambersburg PA
CBHW020307290526
45784CB00003B/1405